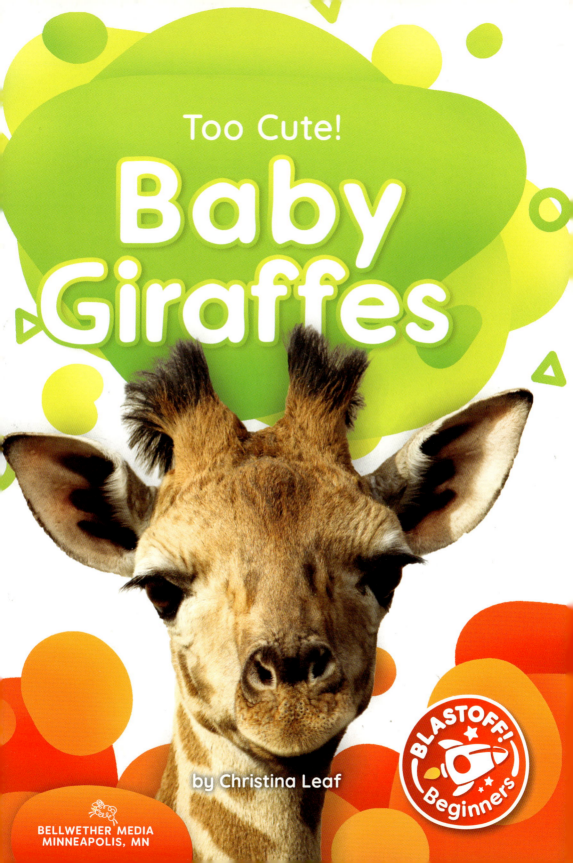

Too Cute!
Baby Giraffes

by Christina Leaf

BLASTOFF! Beginners

BELLWETHER MEDIA
MINNEAPOLIS, MN

Blastoff! Beginners are developed by literacy experts and educators to meet the needs of early readers. These engaging informational texts support young children as they begin reading about their world. Through simple language and high frequency words paired with crisp, colorful photos, Blastoff! Beginners launch young readers into the universe of independent reading.

Sight Words in This Book

are	from	run	up
at	in	than	with
away	look	the	
can	new	them	
eat	people	they	
find	play	to	

This edition first published in 2022 by Bellwether Media, Inc.

No part of this publication may be reproduced in whole or in part without written permission of the publisher. For information regarding permission, write to Bellwether Media, Inc., Attention: Permissions Department, 6012 Blue Circle Drive, Minnetonka, MN 55343.

Library of Congress Cataloging-in-Publication Data

Names: Leaf, Christina, author.
Title: Baby giraffes / by Christina Leaf.
Description: Minneapolis, MN : Bellwether Media, Inc., 2022. | Series: Too cute! | Includes bibliographical references and index. | Audience: Ages 4-7 | Audience: Grades K-1
Identifiers: LCCN 2021040723 (print) | LCCN 2021040724 (ebook) | ISBN 9781644875742 (library binding) | ISBN 9781648345852 (ebook)
Subjects: LCSH: Giraffe--Infancy--Juvenile literature.
Classification: LCC QL737.U56 L433 2022 (print) | LCC QL737.U56 (ebook) | DDC 599.63813/92--dc23
LC record available at https://lccn.loc.gov/2021040723
LC ebook record available at https://lccn.loc.gov/2021040724

Text copyright © 2022 by Bellwether Media, Inc. BLASTOFF! BEGINNERS and associated logos are trademarks and/or registered trademarks of Bellwether Media, Inc.

Editor: Amy McDonald   Designer: Jeffrey Kollock

Printed in the United States of America, North Mankato, MN.

Table of Contents

A Baby Giraffe!	4
With the Herd	12
Growing Up	18
Baby Giraffe Facts	22
Glossary	23
To Learn More	24
Index	24

A Baby Giraffe!

Look at the baby giraffe!
Hello, calf!

Newborn calves can stand up. They are taller than most people!

Newborns are strong. They can run right away!

Calves **nurse**. They stand tall to drink mom's milk.

With the Herd

Giraffes live in **herds**. Herds keep calves safe.

herd

Calves meet friends.
They play.
They run around.

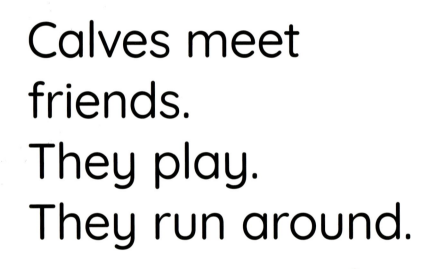

Older calves
eat leaves.
They pull them
from trees.

Growing Up

Calves grow up. Most girl calves stay with the herd.

Most boy calves find new homes. Goodbye, calf!

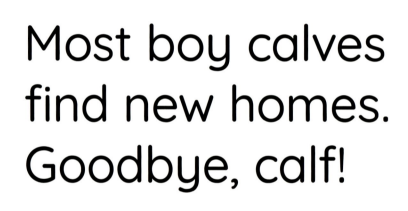

Baby Giraffe Facts

Giraffe Life Stages

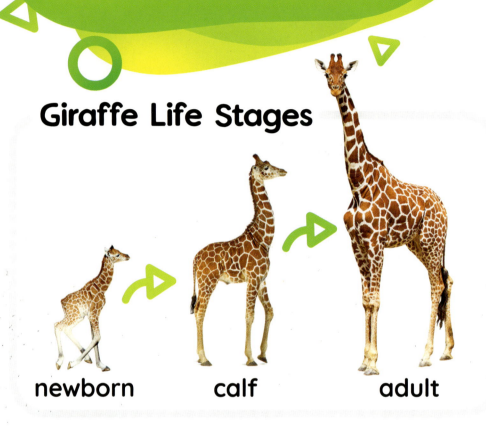

newborn   calf   adult

A Day in the Life

nurse   play   eat leaves

Glossary

herds

groups of giraffes

newborn

just born

nurse

to drink mom's milk

To Learn More

ON THE WEB

FACTSURFER

Factsurfer.com gives you a safe, fun way to find more information.

1. Go to www.factsurfer.com.

2. Enter "baby giraffes" into the search box and click 🔍.

3. Select your book cover to see a list of related content.

Index

boys, 20
drink, 10
eat, 16
friends, 14
giraffe, 4
girls, 18
grow, 18
herds, 12, 13, 18
homes, 20

leaves, 16
milk, 10
mom, 10
newborn, 6, 8
nurse, 10, 11
people, 6
play, 14
run, 8, 14
stand, 6, 10

tall, 6, 10
trees, 16

The images in this book are reproduced through the courtesy of: Henk Bentlage, front cover; Svetlana Foote, p. 3; Petr Bonek, pp. 4, 22 (newborn); John Michael Vosloo, p. 5; Lori Ellis/ Alamy, pp. 6-7; Mees Kuiper, pp. 8-9; Artush, pp. 10-11; jaroslava V, p. 12; Craig Fraser, pp. 12-13; Christian Musat, p. 14; Henk Bogaard, pp. 14-15, 23 (herd); ttomasek15, pp. 16-17; William T Smith, pp. 18-19; Dmussman, p. 20; assalve, pp. 20-21; Eric Isselee, p. 22 (calf); Kotomiti Okuma, p. 22 (adult); Kitch Bain, p. 22 (nurse); Dave Pusey, p. 22 (play); MyImages - Micha, p. 22 (eat); Mary Ann McDonald, p. 23 (newborn); Kobus Peche, p. 23 (nurse).